WRITE IT MAKE IT PLAIN...

Vision

WRITE IT MAKE IT PLAIN
Copyright © 2015 by Shakisha Edness
Published by T.R.A.C Publishing

Cover design: Google and Cover Creator
Editor: Shanice Edness
Interior illustration: Google
Interior design: T.R.A.C Publishing
Bible Scriptures: New Living Translation
ISBN: 10: 069233629
ISBN: 13: 978-0692363621
Library of Congress catalog card number:
Printed in the United States of America

DEDICATION

This book is written exclusively to every man that has a vision to be released through his loins and to every woman that needs to birth a vision through her womb. A vision, testimony, and/or experience that they would like to share with the world.

Writing a book is not just writing a story to make a profit. It is a ministry! Yes, that's exactly what it is. So I have written this book just for you. Allowing the Holy Spirit to speak through me so that you may take the desire, that is placed in you, seriously.

Do not allow that of which is designed to save and change a life, be watered down by thinking you are only writing a book to make money! No, that is not true. People, of which you'll never get a chance to meet, will be inspired by you. You will be used to guide, nurture, educate, and transform lives through your story.

I pray that the anointing of the Holy Spirit come alive in you, begin to stir up your gift, and allow you to write the vision and make it plain. And that it blesses someone who will read it, and run with it!

Have no fear, the Lord Jesus Christ is near and dear. He will guide you along the way. And as you delight yourself in Him, He will give you the desires of your heart.

God said that He will supply ALL of your needs according to His riches and His Glory. Amen. So do not worry about what you do not have, but be concerned with what you do have.

"You have enough left to finish the assignment that is on your life." - Bishop Dale C. Bronner.

ACKNOWLEDGEMENTS

I give thanks to my creator, father, friend, keeper, provider, way maker, teacher, preacher, and every other title you want to use for Our Father that loves us unconditionally and that created us for His purpose.

God you said, "You knew me before I was created in my mother's womb." You knew what I was designed to do and more importantly to be. You have ordered my steps and you constantly provide my needs to complete the work that you have designed me to do.

Thank you for your plans for my life to prosper and do me no harm, for hope, and a future.

Lord, the same way you allowed my father's seed to flow through his loins, connected it with my mother's egg, and allowed the embryo to develop me. That's is the exact same way that you have allowed your gift to be birthed through me.

I thank you for using my gift. Creating me to be a midwife to others in order to help them birth their vision in Jesus' name Amen.

Father God, thank you for the supporters that you provided to support me through. Thanks a lot for the encouragers that encouraged me through. Also, the one's you sent to lift me when I was down during the process of birthing out the bundle of Joy.

Now God, I know you are not a respecter of a person. Meaning what you do for one you will do for all. God thank you in advance for those that will take the vision that is written plain, that they will understand it and run with it to birth out what is lying dormant in them, in Jesus's name Amen.

CONTENTS

The contents in this book will instruct you on how to self – publish your book(s), that are taking residency in you. Imagine the doctor just giving you the news that you are expecting a baby. Regardless if you are the mother or father to the child, you must prepare for the arrival before the due date.

Now you are aware that a baby is soon to come and the due date has been set. The most important thing to know is that you have three choices. One, you can abort the vision. Two, miscarry. Three, birth the vision! I pray that one and two is NOT an option!

We are aware that it takes nine months to deliver a baby. We are NOT having any premature babies either!

The mother and father has to prepare emotionally, mentally, physically, spiritually, socially, and financially for their new arrival. But while the parents are preparing for the baby, the child is being nurtured while in the mother's womb.

Allow the contents to minister and nurture you through the process of preparing to deliver your healthy vision, testimony, and gift to the world.

Let the words penetrate through you and equip you in Jesus' name Amen.

"The only Vision that is aborted is the one that is not birthed."
~ Author Shakisha Edness

INTRO

You are pregnant! Yes, you have just been given the positive results. Let's stay positive about this matter. No need to panic. The world will soon see your vision, hold it, and sow a seed into it by purchasing it. But the most important thing about today is knowing what to do so you can have a healthy baby.

Did I say congratulations? Congratulations! I am Dr. Edness. You will be under my care for the next several months. Please listen and follow my instructions. Midwife Shakisha will assist me during this process.

I want you to take your vitamins and iron pills, eat your fruits, vegetables, and drink plenty of water. Milk and orange juice does your body good and helps the baby develop well.

I am sure you are excited and I am excited for you! Just relax and do as you're instructed to do and I promise we will soon be delivering your precious seed and the rest is Legacy.

"History dies before you. But your Legacy lives long after you."
— Author Shakisha Edness

Revelation 12:11
"And they have defeated him by the Blood of the Lamb and by their testimony. And they did not love their lives so much that they were afraid to die."

We overcome by the Blood of the Lamb and the sharing of our testimonies. Many of us have lived through many trials and tribulations, but we have not shared it with anyone else to help them come out of their storm. The Word of God instructs us to do so. Some will share on platforms, collectively, and/or individually. Others will share their experiences through messages and/or books. The people that you cannot or will not ever meet in person, has an opportunity to overcome by someone sharing their testimony through books.

Never rebel the Holy Spirit when He instructs you to share, regardless of where you are or to who you are speaking with; because you never know whose life is straddling the fence of suicidal thoughts.

Be quick to share at all times. Yes, be careful with who you share your information with, because you do not want to share with any and everybody. You do not want to use it to manipulate others either. But when God says share or a certain testimony of yours comes to your remembrance, while ministering or testifying to another, please share.

Be courageous and free, know that there's only one God that can judge you or place you. You have nothing to be afraid or ashamed of. Amen.

So imagine yourself being filled with many testimonies that you know can be helpful to someone else. Now here's your opportunity to get it out of your head, into the form of a book, and then on a platform for others to read. Share the knowledge and wisdom that you have.

It's your time to make it known, in Jesus' name Amen!

Habakkuk 2:2
"Then the LORD said to me, "Write my answer plainly on tablets, so that a runner can carry the correct message to others."

The way to write is to share from your heart, experiences, and beliefs. No one can take from you or your truth, though sometimes your truth is not true to others. But your experiences are yours and whatever you learned from them is worth sharing. Your beliefs are yours as well, but someone out there may believe what you believe or just need a new perception; so share.

"Always allow your heart to speak as loud as you allowed it to cry." – Author Shakisha Edness.

One's heart always has the ability to reach another's heart. I never try to speak like anyone else. I speak from my heart to the one that has opened the door for me to come in, and hears me loud and clear.

Never get caught up into how long your story must be. I once heard a wise man say, *"The Strength is not in its Length!" – Bishop Dale C. Bronner*

So the first step to writing your vision and making it plain, is writing from the core of your heart, experiences, and beliefs. Not being concerned on how long the text is, but more concerned with the weight of the message.

Many are afraid, because they feel no one wants to hear what they have to say.

The best way to fight fear is to face it! Face your fear by introducing faith! Yes, Peter was not in the boat alone, but Peter took a Faith Walk on Water alone. Amen.

Let your voice be heard by writing your truth.

Proverbs 4:23
"Guard your heart above all else, for it determines the course of your life."

Guard everything that is in your heart! That simply means that you should trust no one with your work before you copyright it. Yes, you must write the vision, make it plain, and then protect it!

Go to www.copyright.gov and register your text for thirty-five dollars. You would rather be protected and nothing ever happen, than not to be and cannot prove that the literature belongs to you.

Your book is your baby and it must go through a process of birthing it. You do not want to miscarry or abort the vision, so protect it with all diligence!

Imagine having a household full of merchandise that cannot be replaced. Would you leave it on the front porch or with the door unlocked and wide open? No, of course not! You will be the security on guard at all times. Much like guarding that winning lottery ticket; you wouldn't risk losing it or someone stealing it. So that's exactly how you have to be over your books.

Your books are a part of your legacy and they are your Gifts. God's Word states, "Your Gifts will make room for you." Guard your Gift!

Isaiah 45:2
"This is what the LORD says: "I will go before you, Cyrus, and level the mountains. I will smash down gates of bronze and cut through bars of iron."

An editor is one of the most important instruments used to bring your vision into fruition! My suggestion to you is to hire someone that knows *your voice* not just words.

Many will say do not allow a friend or family member to edit your work. But I say get a reputable person that is very intelligent and has the ability to speak correctly through your voice.

You do not want someone that comes in and changes your story. You desire to have someone that can strategically and effectively make your work a Masterpiece.

They are used by God to make the crooked words straight. So, build a relationship with someone that you know you can trust. Someone that's dedicated and committed to you and your assignment at hand.

Set goals and deadlines. Remember after the editor is completely finished with the editing process, then you must reread the work from an editor's standpoint. Meaning you're now editing the work of the editor.

If you would like a third person's perspective; ask someone to read the book in its entirety and give their opinion. They will then tell you if they noticed any mistakes or anything they felt needed to be corrected. It's just an opinion, but you have the last say.

In the event you cannot find someone, you can hire someone from www.fiverr.com. Though I have not used site, I do know others who have. But you must do your research on the company yourself.

1Samuel 16:7
But the LORD said to Samuel, "Don't judge by his appearance or height, for I have rejected him. The LORD doesn't see things the way you see them. People judge by outward appearance, but the LORD looks at the heart."

You have been taught to never judge a book by its cover, though many people do. That's why it's very important for you to hire the next most important tool used to help you make a fashion statement in the book industry, a graphic designer.

Now this is much like you getting dressed in the morning for a television interview. You want to dress to impress. Because what you're trying to do is attract others to pick up your book and purchase it, before reading the contents inside.

There are a couple of options here. You can hire a graphic designer that you know or you can go to www.fiverr.com. Also, you can purchase images for your book cover from www.shutterstock.com and can create the book cover yourself with cover creator.

The most important information is to make sure you have a cover that explains the purpose of the book.

I must stress, I haven't used www.fiverr.com. However, I was highly considering using this site. So please research websites I have provided in this book, before using them. These are only options that are available to you.

The title to your book is much like putting on your perfume or cologne to enhance the cover. Make sure it's catchy!

Exodus 35:31-32
"The LORD has filled Bezalel with the Spirit of God, giving him great wisdom, ability, and expertise in all kinds of crafts. He is a master craftsman, expert in working with gold, silver, and bronze."

Formatting your book can be one of the hardest or easiest of the necessary steps. But to keep everything simple, simply download a pre-formatted template. You can type the book into it as you go or you can copy and paste it into the template.

If you are very good at formatting, go for it yourself! For instructions to learn how; go to YouTube and search "how to format my book" or go to www.fiverr.com.

The templates work just fine.

Choosing a font is a total different topic. But choose the one you like, then after you receive the proof you can decided if it works for you. If not, change it.

The size of the book is totally up to you, there are many standard sizes to choose from.

The main key to self-publishing your book is this, it is your vision, your story, so be unique by designing the interior and exterior the way you want to!

Do not try to duplicate anyone's work attempting to get noticed. Because if it's already there, why would I purchase another one?

1 Corinthians 14:40
"But be sure that everything is done properly and in order."

After you have written and copyrighted the book; the book has been edited, formatted, and cover designed. You must get your book an ISBN.

The **ISBN (International Standard Book Number)** is a 10- or 13-digit number used for identification. An **ISBN** is unique to every book, so it is the best way to find the exact edition of the book you're looking for.

You have three options to obtaining this number. You can get it for free but you cannot be listed as the Publisher, or you can purchase it for ten dollars and be listed as the Publisher. Also, you have an option of purchasing them in bulk.

I suggest that you read the fine print with the company that I will list at the end of this book. Again it depends on whether or not you are going to start your own Small Press Publishing Company.

Proverbs 18:16
"Giving a gift can open doors; it gives access to important people!"

God's Word said, "Your gift will make room for you and bring you before Great men." With that being said, you may have many books in you that has been lying dormant; so you may want to start you a Small Press Publishing Company.

That is exactly what I did. I decided to start my own Small Press Publishing Company because, I have too many books inside of me that need to be birthed through me.

If you decide to do the same thing, make sure you apply for your business license, EIN through the IRS, and make sure your business name is available. These are a few basic needs that you will need to cover.

Always ask questions and do your research. Every state differs.

1 Thessalonians 5:21
"But test everything that is said. Hold on to what is good."

.

When the book is completed along with obtaining the ISBN, now it's time that you must order the proof copy. Sit down and read the book thoroughly and carefully. Correct what needs to be corrected.

Then, go to the website and click Approved. Now make a Joyful noise unto the Lord, because you are now officially an Author!

Yes, you are an Author! God said, "He will make your name great."

Genesis 12:2
"I will make you into a great nation. I will bless you and make you famous, and you will be a blessing to others."

Psalm 34:8
"Taste and see that the LORD is good. Oh, the joys of those who take refuge in him!"

You are now a *Self-Published Author!* Be the first to order a few copies and share with your family and friends. Prepare to plan your first book signing.

Trust God to guide your footsteps along the way, because this process will be a journey. But trust God and take Him at His word.

Jeremiah 29:11
"For I know the plans I have for you," says the LORD. "They are plans for good and not for disaster, to give you a future and a hope."

Be noticed on the Top IV Platforms tomorrow!

Ingram Book Company

BAKER & TAYLOR

amazon.com

BARNES & NOBLE
BOOKSELLERS

Self-Publish and Distribute Your Books Through

CREATESPACE

Set up your account today!

If you are interested in a class and/or our services
Please contact
T.R.A.C Publishing Company
At
P.O Box 1243
Austell, Georgia 30168

Or
Email us at
trac.pub@gmail.com

T.R.A.C Publishing stands for Truth Reveals Actions Change. If the Truth is Revealed, One's Actions Should Change.

We are fully staffed and equipped to cover all your needs. We are capable of publishing poetry, children books, fiction, and nonfiction books.

We encourage all to do the work themselves if this is something they have time to do, in order to save money. But we are ready, willing, and able to teach a hands-on class for those that want the service provided for them.

We hope that the information provided brings your Vision into Fruition, in Jesus' name Amen.

"Books are spoken words of ministry from one heart to another. Allow your heart to speak life, and help the beats of their hearts Beat again."
Author Shakisha Edness

www.ingramcontent.com/pod-product-compliance
Lightning Source LLC
Chambersburg PA
CBHW070723210326
41520CB00016B/4437